WORLD OF
MAMMALS

SEA OTTERS

by Sophie Lockwood

Content Adviser: Barbara E. Brown, Associate, Mammal Division, The Field Museum, Chicago, IL

THE CHILD'S WORLD®, CHANHASSEN, MINNESOTA

SEA OTTERS

Published in the United States of America by The Child's World®
PO Box 326 • Chanhassen, MN 55317-0326 • 800-599-READ • www.childsworld.com

Acknowledgements:

The Child's World®: Mary Berendes, Publishing Director

Editorial Directions, Inc.: E. Russell Primm, Editorial Director; Pam Rosenberg, Editor; Judith Shiffer, Assistant Editor; Matt Messbarger, Editorial Assistant; Susan Hindman, Copy Editor; Emily Dolbear, Proofreader; Judith Frisbie and Olivia Nellums, Fact Checkers; Tim Griffin/IndexServ, Indexer; Cian Loughlin O'Day, Photo Researcher, Linda S. Koutris, Photo Editor

The Design Lab: Kathleen Petelinsek, Designer, Production Artist, and Cartographer

Photos:

Cover: Joel W. Rogers/Corbis; half title/CIP: Ralph A Clevenger/Corbis; frontispiece: Brandon D. Cole/Corbis.

Interior: Animals Animals/Earth Scenes: 19 (Rich Reid), 23 (Enlightened Images); Corbis: 5-middle left and 16, 5-bottom left and 29 (Werner Forman), 10 (Brandon D. Cole), 14 (Ray Corral), 30 (Genevieve Naylor), 35 (Jonathan Blair); Getty Images: 5-top right and 9 (Stone/Chuck Davis) 32 (AFP/Chris Wilkins); Photodisc: 5-bottom right and 27, 13, 25; Kennan Ward/Corbis: 5-top left and 7, 36.

Library of Congress Cataloging-in-Publication Data

Lockwood, Sophie.
  Sea otters / by Sophie Lockwood.
     p. cm. — (The world of mammals)
  Includes index.
  ISBN 1-59296-500-8 (lib. bdg. : alk. paper) 1. Sea otter—Juvenile literature.
I. Title. II. World of mammals (Chanhassen, Minn.)
  QL737.C25L63 2005
  599.769'5—dc22   2005000568

TABLE OF CONTENTS

Chapter One

The Big Surprise

In 1741, Danish explorer Vitus Bering was leading an **expedition** to map the Pacific coast of Russia. Bad luck left Bering shipwrecked on an Alaskan island, and he died. Some of his crew eventually returned to the court of the Russian czar, or ruler. They brought with them remarkably fine furs—sea otter skins. That was the start of 170 years of nonstop hunting that caused the near **extinction** of sea otters.

Early in the 1700s, more than 20,000 sea otters lived, played, and fed in California's coastal **kelp** beds. Hundreds of thousands of sea otters swam in the icy waters off Alaska, Russia, and northern Japan. But when sea otter fur became fashionable, these animals were doomed.

By the early 1900s, fur-taking had seriously decreased the seal and otter populations throughout the Pacific Ocean. Sea otters had already become extinct in the California waters because of extensive hunting. None had been seen since 1831. **Conservation** was

Would You Believe?
Sea otter fur has 93,000 to 155,000 hairs per square centimeter (600,000 to 1 million sq. in.) That is the densest fur of any animal. How many hairs are on your head? About 100,000 to 150,000.

Sea otter fur was highly prized and led to the overhunting of these playful creatures.

necessary if these furbearing mammals were to survive. So in 1911, Great Britain, Russia, Japan, and the United States signed the Fur Seal Treaty. The treaty banned the hunting of fur seals and sea otters. But was the treaty too late to save those species?

On March 19, 1938, Howard Granville Sharpe was in for a big surprise. Sharpe lived on the Pacific coast near Carmel, California. He often used a telescope to scan the waters beneath the cliffs of Big Sur. That morning, he noticed some creatures floating in the kelp beds. What could they be? He thought of seals, sea lions, or even walruses, but it wasn't any of those animals. Sharpe was looking at sea otters. Unfortunately, no one believed him. Sea otters in California? Impossible! There hadn't been any for 100 years. It was like claiming dinosaurs walked the streets of New York.

Sharpe finally convinced Captain Lippincott of the California Fish and Game Commission to take a look. Lippincott agreed that the creatures were sea otters. To this day, no one has ever figured out where the 300 otters came from. Now, about 2,800 sea otters live off of California's coast. These otters are **descendants** of the 300 otters that surprised Sharpe that day in 1938.

Chapter Two

A Keystone Species

Sea otters are considered a keystone species of the kelp forest. A keystone species performs a job in its **ecosystem** that helps other plants and animals survive. Kelp forests provide a nursery for hundreds of fish species, but sea

Kelp are large seaweeds that grow in cold seas. They are part of the group of plantlike organisms known as algae.

urchins feed on kelp and can destroy a kelp forest. Luckily, sea otters, as well as asteroid starfish, feed on urchins. Sea otters keep kelp beds strong and healthy by controlling the sea urchin population.

When sea otters disappear from kelp forests, the area becomes an **aquatic** desert. The kelp die, and fish lose their nursery sites. Even urchins leave because their food supply

Sea urchins feed on kelp.

is gone. Loss of sea otters in the state of Washington and the Canadian province of British Columbia created marine wastelands just off the coast. Reintroduction of sea otters in those regions encouraged new growth of kelp forests and brought new sea life to offshore waters.

Although the kelp ecosystem needs sea otters to thrive, the fishing industry opposes expanding the mammal's territories. Fishers worry that more sea otters in their waters will mean smaller catches of clams and abalone, two animals that sea otters feed on. They must remember that, without sea otters, the coastal area might become an aquatic desert with no clams or abalone at all.

THE SMALLEST MARINE MAMMAL

Sea otters are the smallest of the marine mammals, a group that includes whales, dolphins, seals, sea lions, and walruses. Baby otters drink mother's milk when they are born. Though they often rest on land, sea otters could spend their entire lives in the water. Sea otters rarely go farther than 2 kilometers (1.2 mi) from the shore. They mate, give birth, feed, and sleep floating above the kelp.

Adult otters measure about 1.5 meters (5 feet) from head to tail. Their

Would You Believe?
Otters have sharp senses. They can see well both above and below the water. Their sense of touch is remarkable. Even their whiskers can sense the slightest vibrations in the water.

tails alone average about 0.3 meter (1 ft) in length. Otter weights vary greatly. Females reach weights between 16 and 27 kilograms (35 and 60 pounds). Males are larger, averaging 23 to 41 kilograms (50 to 90 lbs). Male Alaskan sea otters grow slightly larger, reaching about 45 kilograms (100 lbs).

Sea otter coloring can be any shade from black to pale brown. Older otters have silver-gray fur on their heads. Sea otters also sport exceptionally fine whiskers, which earn them the nickname Old Men of the Sea.

The sea otter is among the few animals that use tools. A sea otter's short front legs and paws are equipped with **retractable** claws. It uses its claws when feeding. A sea otter uses stones to crack open the shells of its favorite foods. Floating on its back with a rock on its chest, the otter taps a clam or sea urchin against the stone to break its shell. These shell-cracking skills are very important because a sea otter needs to eat an amount of food equal to one-fourth of its body weight each day!

EXCELLENT INSULATION

A sea otter's fur, also known as its pelage, is its most outstanding asset. Like many furred mammals, otters have thick, two-layered fur. The underfur is short and dense,

and provides a blanket against the cold. Even though the sea otter lives in water, its underfur is so thick that its skin never gets wet. The outer hairs, called guard hairs, are long, coarse, and brown.

Sea otters spend a great deal of time grooming their fur. They must keep their coats absolutely clean. As they groom, air is pushed between the hairs. The air cushion helps insulate the otter from the cold.

Oil spills are very dangerous for sea otters. The

A sea otter's fur keeps it warm and dry, even when the animal spends much of its time in the water.

Would You Believe?
Most marine mammals—
sea lions, seals, whales, and
walruses—have thick layers of
blubber to keep them warm.
Sea otters have none. They
need only their fur to stay
warm in the frigid waters of
the northern Pacific.

otters' coats get mat-
ted with oil and cannot
be cleaned. Soiled coats
cannot keep otters dry
or protect them from the
cold. As a result, they die
from **hypothermia.**

A volunteer takes care of a sea otter rescued after an oil spill.

Chapter Three

In the Kelp Forest

In Glacier Bay, Alaska, a young sea otter pup is born. Infants can be born at any time, but in Alaska, most arrive in late spring. His eyes are open, and he has a full set of teeth.

The newborn sea otter pup depends on his mother for survival. At birth, he weighs between 1.4 and 2.3 kilograms (3 and 5 lbs). Most of the time, the pup rides on its mother's chest. Although he will live most of his life in the water, he cannot swim at birth. He will not learn to swim until he is one month old. He will learn to dive at two months old.

Sea otters make excellent mothers, but even the best mothers get hungry. The mother leaves her baby alone while she hunts for food. Before she dives for abalone or sea urchins, she wraps her pup with kelp. The baby otter's fur is filled with air, which helps keep him afloat. The kelp provides a security blanket for the pup.

Sea otter pups remain infants until they are about six months old. At that

Would You Believe?
Sea otter pups are sometimes eaten by bald eagles. The birds swoop down and take pups that are floating alone in the water while their mothers hunt.

A sea otter pup spends much of its time floating on its mother's chest.
Pups learn to swim when they are about one month old.

point, they are considered **juveniles.** From then until they are one year old, juveniles still depend on their mothers. Many continue to drink mother's milk. During this time, their mothers teach them what to eat and where to find food. They weigh about 14 kilograms (30 lbs) when they are **weaned.**

From one to three years of age, young sea otters are considered **subadults.** They no longer depend on their mothers and can hunt for themselves. They have the skills of adult sea otters, but they are not old enough to produce young.

A female sea otter usually has her first pup by the time she is five years old. From then on, she will produce one pup about every two years.

Otters live in groups called rafts or pods. A raft may have as few as 2 or as many as 1,000 or more sea otters. The raft's size depends on several factors. The main factor is the amount of food in the area. It takes a huge number of clams, abalone, urchins, and fish to feed 1,000 otters.

When a raft outgrows its territory, adventurous males take off to look for a new place to

live. Adult male explorers may cover 100 kilometers (62 mi) or more in just a few days. When a possible new home is found, the adventurers move in and take over the kelp forest, rocks, or tidewater stones.

Male sea otters usually live about ten to fifteen years in the wild. Females tend to live longer—about fifteen to twenty years. Disease, old age, and **predators** account for most sea otter deaths. The most common predators of the sea otter are great white sharks and killer whales, or orcas.

Sea otters spend nearly eleven hours a day frolicking, resting, or sleeping. Otters are playful and enjoy a good game with their friends. To make sure they don't drift away while sleeping, otters wrap themselves in kelp. Kelp **fronds** make sturdy anchors.

Another five hours a day is spent grooming. A sea otter cannot be sloppy about its coat. Grooming must be thorough to make sure every bit of fur on the otter's body is cleaned.

The remaining time each day is spent hunting for food. Sea otters hunt at any time, night or day. They have fast **metabolisms** and must eat regularly. They use nutrition quickly and must keep their bodies well fed to stay warm and healthy.

Would You Believe?
Sea otters are backstroke experts. They have powerful hind flippers that propel them through the water on their backs.

Chapter Four

The Otter Family

The scientific name for sea otters is *Enhydra lutris.*
Sea otters have only one species but several subspecies.
Identified subspecies of sea otters include Southern or

An Alaskan sea otter relaxes in a fjord off southern Alaska's Kenai Peninsula.

Would You Believe?
The Southern, or Californian, sea otter is listed as threatened in the wild.

Californian, Alaskan, Russian, and Asian or Japanese. Some scientists question whether the Asian sea otter is a true subspecies.

For the most part, all sea otter subspecies look alike, eat the same foods, and follow the same daily routine. Location and population size are what distinguishes the different subspecies.

The Southern sea otter population steadily increased in size from 1938 to 1995. The otters continued to build new colonies southward toward Los Angeles and Santa Barbara Island. Scientists were delighted, but fishing fleets were not. The fishing industry complained that the sea otters hurt fishing in the region.

Government officials tried to control the movement

Where Sea Otters Are Found

Subspecies	Scientific name	Range
Southern or Californian	*Enhydra lutris nereis*	Santa Barbara to Half Moon Bay, California
Asian or Japanese	*Enhydra lutris gracilis*	Hokkaido Island, Japan
Russian	*Enhydra lutris lutris*	Kurile Islands north to Commander Islands, Russia
Alaskan or northern	*Enhydra lutris kenyoni*	Washington coast to tip of Aleutian Islands

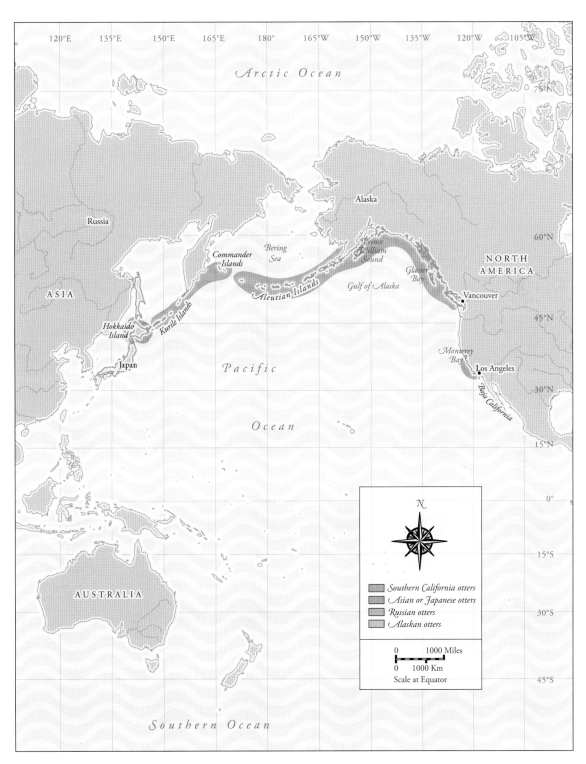

Sea otters live in the Pacific Ocean off the coasts of North America and Asia.
The largest populations live in the Pacific's cold, northernmost waters.

The Channel Islands off California's southern coast are rugged and mountainous.

of the otters. They introduced new otter colonies on California's Channel Islands. They also tried to develop an otter-free zone. These programs attempted to restrain the otters' natural **instincts.**

Unfortunately, the Channel Islands colonies failed. The otter-free zone also didn't work. Otters wanted to hunt where food was plentiful, not where humans wanted them to. The otter-free zone idea was abandoned. Today's plan for the California sea otter allows the animals to roam freely and restricts the fishing industry instead.

The largest sea otter population lives between Washington State and the Aleutian Islands of Alaska. That population is also changing. In recent years, the number of otters living in the Aleutian Islands has decreased by 90 percent. In the 1980s, the Aleutian population was estimated at 100,000.

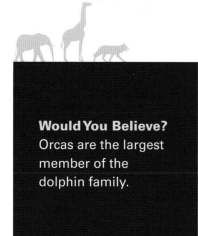

Today, there are fewer than 9,000 sea otters there.

The decline may be due to several things. One possibility is that orcas have begun preying on sea otters. Though orcas prefer seals and sea lions, scientists believe that reduced numbers of these prey have forced the killer whales to hunt sea otters. Other possible causes are pollution and disease.

Along Alaska's southeastern coast, the sea otter news is quite different. Otter rafts are increasing by huge numbers. Officials hope to find ways to control their growth rate.

One way of handling the mushrooming numbers may be to set up new otter territories. At one time, Washington State and Canada's British Columbia had many sea otter colonies. Hunting destroyed those populations. Between 1969 and 1972, scientists reestablished otter colonies in Washington and Vancouver, British Columbia.

The Washington population began with 59 otters. Today, that population stands at more than 500 animals and is still growing. The Vancouver experiment began with 89 animals and reached 1,500 otters by 1995. These successful programs may encourage relocating sea otter pods that are currently overpopulating areas such as Glacier Bay, Alaska.

THE MUSTELID FAMILY: WEASELS, OTTERS, AND MINKS

Sea otters belong to the Mustelid family. Other family members include weasels, river otters, minks, badgers, ferrets, and skunks. Sea otters are most similar to river otters.

River otters come in two varieties: the river otter and

Like its relative the sea otter, the mink is highly prized for its fur.

Chapter Five

The Past, The Present, and The Future

Scientists believe that sea otters have existed for 1 million to 3 million years. Their original range began as far south as Baja California and ran up the coast to the Aleutians, across the Bering Sea to the Commander Islands and south to northern Japan.

Most native tribes living along the northern Pacific coast depended in some way on sea otters. They hunted otters for meat and fur. Sea otter pelts were prized for their softness and warmth. But the number of sea otters killed by Natives was small. Even today, native tribes in Alaska are allowed to hunt enough sea otters to fill their basic needs.

Would You Believe?
Long ago, Native Americans known as the Athabascans both honored and feared the sea otter. They believed that sea otters were living versions of the souls of humans who had drowned in the ocean.

A Native American artist created this sea otter bowl.

A woman wears an otter fur coat. After years of being hunted for their fur, sea otters were in danger of becoming extinct.

It was only when the Russians arrived in Alaska and discovered the value of sea otter fur that trouble began. After 170 years of constant hunting, so few otters remained that hunting was no longer profitable. The nations involved in sea otter and seal fur hunting signed a treaty to stop the hunting of furbearing marine mammals. That was just the first conservation plan to save the sea otter from extinction.

RECOVERY PLANS

Two major conservation programs safeguard sea otters and their habitats within the United States: the Marine Mammal Protection Act of 1972 (MMPA) and the Endangered Species Act. The MMPA covers a wide range of mammals including sea otters, walruses, dugongs, manatees, polar bears, sea lions, seals, whales, and dolphins. The law prohibits the hunting, injuring, capturing, or bothering of marine mammals in any way. The Endangered Species Act covers hundreds of animals and plants in every environment from the desert to the sea. Southern sea otters are listed as threatened on the Endangered Species List.

Individual states have also passed laws to protect sea otters. California law forbids fishing with **gill nets** close to the shore. These fishing nets often catch more than fish.

Cleanup workers scrub rocks in Prince William Sound after the 1989 oil spill.

Sea otters, seals, sea turtles, dolphins, and other marine creatures get tangled in gill nets and die. The first California gill net law in 1980 prohibited use of the nets in waters less than 55 meters (180 ft) deep. That depth was increased to 110 meters (360 ft) in 2001 because otters had to feed in deeper waters because of pollution, overfishing, and human activity.

THREATS TO SURVIVAL

Another serious threat to sea otter survival is pollution. In Alaska's Prince William Sound, a massive oil spill occurred in March 1989. Oil spread over the water, creating an environmental disaster. Volunteers desperately tried to clean the oil from otter fur and bird feathers. Despite their efforts, many animals died. More than 1,000 otter bodies washed ashore.

Another pollution-related problem is runoff. Fertilizer, pesticides, and other chemicals build up on land. Water from rain or **irrigation** pours over the land

and washes into storm drains or sewers, eventually emptying into the ocean. This runoff carries those chemicals to the sea. Although otters do not eat the chemicals directly, they end up in otter bodies. Runoff chemicals are taken in by **filter feeders** such as clams, abalone, and mussels. Polluted water passes through their bodies and leaves chemical pollutants behind. When otters eat those shellfish, they also eat the poisonous pollutants.

Scientists keep a close watch on otter populations. They estimate that a total population of 3,000 Southern sea otters, for example, is needed to preserve the species. Up to 1995, the population grew at an even pace. Then, from 1995 to 2004, Southern sea otter populations showed reduced pup births and other worrisome losses. The total population in 1995 was 2,377 animals, including 282 pups. Four years later, the otter count showed only 2,090 otters. Happily, numbers have slowly bounced back, and 2004 proved to be a boom year. The 2004 count showed 2,825 otters, including 330 pups. That is

*Orphaned sea otters learn how to swim at the
Monterey Bay Aquarium in California.*

Sea otters rest while anchored in kelp off the coast of Monterey, California.

the highest Southern otter count since the 1830s.

After studying the problem for the past 100 years, scientists have discovered the best way to preserve sea otters—leave them alone! Otters don't fare well when humans interfere in their environments. Efforts to protect the sea otter must address the problems that humans create. But why should protecting the sea otters be a priority?

The answer is easy. Nature works best in balance. Sea otters restore the natural balance needed for kelp forests to thrive. A thriving kelp forest is also an active nursery for many fish species. If humans hope to harvest the riches of the seas, they need to understand how otters help maintain a healthy, life-giving source of that food. Those playful, furry creatures that bob in the waters above kelp forests are crucial to a balanced ecosystem.

Glossary

aquatic (uh-KWAT-ik) refers to being in water

conservation (kon-sur-VAY-shuhn) the act of saving or preserving some aspect of wildlife

descendants (di-SEND-uhnts) animals that come from a specific ancestor

ecosystem (EE-koh-sis-tuhm) a community of living things and their interactions with the environment

expedition (ek-spuh-DISH-uhn) a special journey

extinction (ek-STINGKT-shuhn) the state of a type of plant or animal no longer existing

filter feeders (FILL-tur FEED-uhrs) animals that get nourishment from the water that passes through their bodies

fronds (FRONDZ) a large leaf on a plant

gill nets (GIL NETS) nets which catch fish by the gills

hypothermia (hye-poh-THUR-mee-uh) a lower-than-normal body temperature

instincts (IN-stingkts) one's natural sense of what one should do or feel

irrigation (ihr-uh-GAY-shuhn) supplying water to crops

juveniles (JOO-vuh-nuhlz) individuals that resemble their parents except in size and ability to produce young

kelp (KELP) a large, brown seaweed

metabolisms (muh-TAB-uh-liz-uhmz) the bodily processes of turning food into energy

predators (PREH-duh-turz) animals that hunt and kill other animals for food

retractable (re-TRAK-tuh-buhl) something that can be drawn or pulled back in

savannas (suh-VAN-uhz) a nearly treeless, flat, grassy plain

subadults (SUHB-uh-duhlts) individuals that are no longer juveniles but not yet able to produce young

weaned (WEEND) no longer drinking mother's milk

For More Information

Watch It

Beneath the Surface. VHS (Pacific Grove, Calif.: Friends of the Sea Otter, 2000).

Precipice of Survival: The Southern Sea Otter. Online Video, *http://online.wr.usgs.gov/outreach/* (U.S. Department of the Interior, U.S. Geological Survey, 2004).

Read It

Murray, Peter. *Sea Otters.* Chanhassen, Minn.: The Child's World, 2001.

Smith, Roland. *Sea Otter Rescue: The Aftermath of an Oil Spill.* New York: Puffin Books, 1999.

Springer, Susan Woodward, and Amy Meissner (illustrator). *Seldovia Sam and the Sea Otter Rescue.* Anchorage: Alaska Northwest Books, 2003.

VanBlaricom, Glenn R. *Sea Otters.* Stillwater, Minn.: Voyageur Press, 2001.

Look It Up

Visit our home page for lots of links about sea otters: *http://www.childsworld.com/links*

Note to Parents, Teachers, and Librarians: We routinely verify our Web links to make sure they are safe, active sites—so encourage your readers to check them out!

The Animal Kingdom
Where Do Sea Otters Fit In?

Kingdom: Animal

Phylum: Chordates (animals with backbones)

Class: Mammalia (animals that feed their young milk)

Order: Carnivora (meat-eating animals)

Family: Mustelidae

Genus: *Enhydra*

Species: *lutris*

Subspecies:

    gracilis (Asian or Japanese)

    kenyoni (Alaskan)

    lutris (Russian)

    nereis (Southern or Californian)

Index

About the Author

Sophie Lockwood is a former teacher and a longtime writer. She writes textbooks, newspaper articles, and magazine articles. Sophie enjoys writing about animals and their habits. The most interesting part of her research, Sophie says, is learning how scientists apply their knowledge to save endangered species. She lives with her husband in the foothills of the Blue Ridge Mountains.